For My Son

If it is true that we are judged
By the deeds of the child we bear,
Then I shall truly be a king
When judgement day is here.

George E. Young

Presented to:

_____

_____

By:

_____

_____

Date: _____

Special Message:

_____

_____

_____

_____

_____

_____

_____

_____

_____

_____

THIS BOOK IS DEDICATED with unconditional love to
W. Dustin Young, the author's true friend and only son.

ACKNOWLEDGMENTS

To William Dustin Young, the author's only son, for his part in that special relationship from which the feelings and thoughts expressed in this book evolved. Thank you, my son, for returning my love and for the patience you have with me as a father and as a man. Thank you for being you.

To my wonderful wife who gave her total support while we went broke writing this book.

TABLE OF CONTENTS

PREFACE

The author of this book does not claim to be an accomplished writer, scholar, philosopher or poet. He is simply a father.

It is the author's hope that through this book other parents will find it possible to communicate thoughts and feelings to their sons for which words were not before available.

The special messages expressed herein are applicable to sons of all ages. Whether read by a young boy or mature adult, these messages should be easily understood and remembered. Since the verses make no reference to dates, terminologies or events pertinent to any specific era, the credence of this book's contents should be preserved for generations to come.

This book is divided into three sections, each dealing with a special and important relationship. The first section deals with the parent/son relationship and expresses thoughts and feelings that most every parent has. The second section deals with perspective . . . the relationship that events of today have with the whole of one's life. The third section addresses the relationship that our personal values and priorities have to our lasting happiness.

Though references to theology have been purposely omitted in recognition and respect for varying religious beliefs, the values and principles expressed herein should parallel and compliment the teachings of most organized religions.

Those who receive this book are fortunate, for someone cared enough to give it. Whether actually from a parent, or from another who truly cares, the gift of this book says that the one receiving it is very special.

THE PARENT/SON RELATIONSHIP

The relationship that exists between a parent and son is a powerful bond like none other that either shall experience. The effect this relationship has on both the parent and the son is deep and lasting, yet the very essence of the relationship is often misunderstood.

Being a good parent is a rewarding, yet very difficult task, as is being a good son. There are no schools that can adequately prepare either for the wonderful roles they have. They must learn as they go. They each will make mistakes.

Unlike many relationships, the one between a parent and child begins with deep mutual love and admiration; a love and admiration that is difficult to destroy and can evolve into a lasting and wonderful friendship. As each begins to grow in their role, they begin to realize that the other has faults and weaknesses. There are periods where the goals, desires and attitudes of one may seem foreign to the other. An understanding of these differences is essential.

It is the degree of understanding that determines the effectiveness of our relationships . . . understanding each other . . . understanding understanding . . . understanding misunderstanding. The only way to truly understand is to communicate; to address differences, to tell and show our feelings, to explore misunderstandings together.

The verses that follow communicate feelings that most parents have . . . feelings that promote understanding . . . feelings that are rarely, if ever, expressed.

1

PLEASE KNOW THAT I'M YOUR FRIEND

Sometimes it's hard to write the words
That you, my son, should see.
Or say the things you need to hear,
Or be as I should be.

You grow so fast and learn so much
It's hard for me each day,
To say or do just what is best
To help along the way.

Should I be silent or give advice?
Should I answer yes or no?
Should I have control — set many rules,
Or simply let you go?

One thing is certain . . . I'll make mistakes,
And some'll seem hard to mend.
But if nothing else is clear, my son,
Please know that I'm your friend.

THINGS THAT MATTER

It's often hard to understand
From where the other comes.
It may seem as if we're marching
To the beat of different drums.

The songs I like, some things I do,
The way I cut my hair,
Must seem to you as very dull
Just as the clothes I wear.

Your youth is now . . . a different day
Than days when I was young.
Some things I never dreamed would be
Are things you live among.

But all the things that matter, son,
Are still the same today.
If only those we understand,
The rest shall fade away.

ULTIMATE PLEASURE

After spending four hours in the blowing snow
  Chopping a big pile of wood,
A cup of hot chocolate and a roaring fire
  Would surely feel mighty good.

You've sweat all day in the blistering sun.
  The temperature's a hundred and three.
Won't that cool shower feel awfully good
  With a glass of ice cold tea?

That kind of pleasure seems unsurpassed,
  But it doesn't compare with one.
There is no pleasure like that I feel
  When I get a hug from my son.

THE TEAM

On the day of your birth a team was born
That team was you and I.
The game is life and the field is rough.
The stakes are very high.

Since you were so young, I became coach.
That's how it had to be.
Just understand that I'm learning, too.
Some plays are new to me.

Some days you will see some other coach
Calling plays you'd like to run.
You'll feel playing on the other team
Would certainly be more fun.

But those days will pass, so try to learn
The coach is on your team.
This coach wants only the best for you.
And shares your every dream.

One other thing you need to know,
Else this very team may fall.
The coach may call some plays, my son,
But it's you who carries the ball.

GENERATION GAP

When you were only a wee little chap,
I'd heard about the generation gap.
I swore it would never exist with us.
"Not between me and this cute little cuss."

I tried to stay young and to know your ways;
To learn to appreciate whatever's the craze,
But soon I found that I appear a sap
When I'm on your side of the generation gap.

By the same token, you just wouldn't be you
If you did things the same as I used to do.
So let's face one thing, there's certainly a gap.
It was planned that way, son. It's not a mishap.

It wouldn't be good to look the other way
And pretend that gap doesn't exist today.
Let's explore that gap and try to find out
Just what the other side is all about.

If I can understand from where you come
And let you know where I'm coming from,
Then though time put us on a different ridge,
Mutual understanding will be our bridge.

A BIT MORE CREDIT

"If only parents could understand!"
You must think that quite a lot.
And sometimes, son, I wish we could,
Cause perfect we are not.

But perhaps a bit more credit's due,
Once all the data's compiled,
For you've not been a parent as yet,
But we were once a child.

FOR YOU I WISH

I wish for you a contented life
  Filled with love and grace.
For there is no greater joy for me
  Than a smile upon your face.
But when times get hard and you feel pain,
  I hope that all your pride
Won't keep me from where I'd want to be,
  And that is by your side.

I wish for you a life of great wealth
  If that's for what you yearn.
But if it's not, I'll be just as proud
  No matter what you earn.
For you see, my son, it's not those things
  That set some men apart.
It's not what's in your bank account,
  But what's truly in your heart.

I wish for you a life of your own. . .
  The way you want it to be.
The path you choose and where it may lead
  Will not be up to me.
Wherever you go, whatever you become,
  No matter what you do.
You'll always have my love and support.
  I wish the best for you.

UNCONDITIONAL LOVE

Remember, son, if you're a success,
I'll be happy as can be.
But remember, too, that when you fail,
You can always come to me.

There's little in life we cannot share.
We'll share the bad times, too.
For my love has no conditions, son,
That's what I give to you.

SHARING

When I remember my younger days,
My heart goes out to you.
Cause I remember problems I had
That all young folks go through.

I'd do things wrong, or get in trouble,
Or make a bad grade in school.
Friends would do things that hurt my feelings.
I'd be embarrassed, be a fool.

My heart was broken over loves I lost.
At times I felt lonely and sad.
So you see, my son, most problems you have
Were at one time those that I had.

Being a parent means helping your son,
Cause growing up is hard to do.
Sharing successes is part of the joy.
So is sharing the problems, too.

I want you to do the things that are right,
Like I try to teach you to do.
But it won't always happen and I know that.
I once was a young person, too.

If you make a mistake or simply feel sad,
Nothing could make my day as bright,
As your saying to me; "I have a problem.
Can you help me make it alright?".

BEWARE THE SHADOW

My shadow, son, of it beware.
Don't linger where it's laid.
The man you can be, like a lovely flower,
Won't grow well in the shade.

YOU ARE YOU AND I AM ME

I hope you know I'm not the person
  That I want you to be.
It's important for you to realize
  You are you and I am me.

There are faults I have and deeds I've done
  I'd never wish for you.
But those can be your greatest lessons
  Of what to or not to do.

REGRETTABLE TIMES

You're home from school, you have things to say,
  And you find that I'm not there.
You have some problem and need to talk,
  But I'm still at work somewhere.

Oh, how I'd love to have shared those times.
  Somehow it doesn't seem fair.
That the only times I now regret
  Are the times I wasn't there.

IF IT WEREN'T FOR YOU

It's often so rough, this being a parent,
That if it weren't for you,
I just don't think that I would be able
To ever make it through.

PERSPECTIVE

One essential key to a truly happy life is the acquired ability to put one's life in proper perspective . . . to measure the importance of today's events in relation to the whole of our lives. It is this ability that can help us to establish our priorities and keep them in order . . . to keep our values intact, our attitude positive and our sense of humor about us.

Whether it's a pimple on your cheek the night of the prom or the death of a loved one; whether a serious illness, a fallen career, a divorce or a failing grade in school; troubles, disappointments and hardships are a major part of every life. How we accept and react to such events can well determine our overall happiness, as well as what kind of person we eventually become.

The happiest of men learn to look past the moment, to appreciate and make the most of what they have and to always see the brightest side. They are strong enough to begin again and wise enough to learn much from what has happened. . . .

FINDING THE BEST

Life is fun, but it's sometimes hard.
It's difficult to comprehend
Why some things happen and some things don't,
Why some things have to end.

Don't try too hard to understand.
Don't confuse yourself with why.
Just find the best in every minute.
It's there if you'll just try.

EVERYDAY

To the ones who say "This day is bad",
  I'll reply to them, my son,
"Some never appreciate every day
  Till they almost miss just one".

TROUBLES

"Nobody knows the troubles I know."
　That's a lot of bull!
Compared to the problems many folks have
　Ours are rather dull.

VIEWING THE BRIGHT SIDE

Does the sun come up in the early morn
   And fall in the west at night?
Are things always as they appear to be?
   Is our perspective right?

A revolving earth brings the sun in view.
   The sun doesn't fall or rise.
What first we see's not always what's there.
   There's more than meets the eyes.

In every misfortune that comes our way
   A blessing can be found.
There is good no matter where we are
   If we'll just look around.

The happiest men look beyond what they see
   Till the bright side is in view.
Is your glass half empty or is it half full?
   That is totally up to you.

19

COUNTING YOUR SHEEP

Problems, as my companions, may . . .
Be with me through most of the day,
But blessings are the little sheep
I count at night to go to sleep.

HUMOR

When a joke is told or a prank is pulled
Even lowliest of men can grin.
For humor, then, is so easy to find.
It's not hidden somewhere within.

The common man can look to the past
And laugh about things he sees.
Cause the hurt is gone and who cares now?
Those are only old memories.

The exceptional guy can laugh at a mirror
And take life's worst with a smile.
He's the man who finds humor in everyday life.
It's that kind of man who has style.

. . . The relationship that today has with the rest of our lives is a complex and often misunderstood relationship, for none of us know what tomorrow will bring. Some understanding can be gained, however, by reviewing a portion of life's normal cycle and some of the stages through which we each must pass.

An infant is brought into life totally dependent on others for survival and happiness. With no thought of tomorrow, his physical comfort, food and love seem his only concern.

Every passing day brings the infant new abilities, new challenges and a little less dependency. Soon, as a pre-schooler, the average child in our country now assumes that a degree of physical comfort and nourishment will be provided. He discovers new joys and develops new desires. The new toy, the upcoming Christmas, the hug of approval from mom and dad; these make up his dreams.

The preschooler has a seemingly simple life. His basic needs are provided by others, yet natural disappointments, frustrations and hurts loom as major catastrophes, bringing grief to his life. How is the pre-school child to know that the hurt of a skinned knee will soon heal, that the scolding was given only out of love or that the broken toy will not affect the whole of his life?

Soon reaching adolescence, the growing child begins to feel independence, yet still must be dependent. Since more and more time is spent away from home, mom's or dad's approval is no longer enough. The desire to fit in with his peers becomes a primary motivation.

Now at an awkward stage between childhood and manhood, the adolescent has sexual urges and feels his body maturing. Some bodies mature earlier than others, causing some adolescents embarrassment over a boyish appearance while others appear more "manly." The pressures to be a "man" or to be grown-up are felt for the first time during adolescence.

His thoughts are preoccupied with the girl in class, getting a driver's license, the prom, school grades, summer vacation, the party next week, maturing physically, the big game, what mom and dad will think or do, the school tryouts, but most of all, with fitting in and being accepted. Everything that happens seems all-important. Small events take on giant proportions. It is at this stage that young people begin to deal more independently with loneliness, rejection, male and female relationships, leadership, success, embarrassment, shame and a host of other emotions.

Like the pre-schooler whose broken toy seems a catastrophic event, how is the adolescent to know that his hurts will soon fade? How is he to know that soon nobody will care if the big game was won or if he fit in? How is he to know that those problems he hides inside are the same ones that mom and dad had? How does he know that those things he does to "fit in" or gain acceptance may well cost him dearly for the rest of his life? How does he know how to put life in perspective? . . .

THAT MYTHICAL CRYSTAL BALL

I wish you had a crystal ball,
But not to see tomorrow...
To go there and look back at now
To better gauge your sorrow.

The weight of grief can crush a man
If he can't look past today,
But grief's like ice and time's the heat
That melts such weight away.

That sadness, son, that breaks your heart
Might'nt seem so big at all,
If you could see it in perspective
Through that mythical crystal ball.

IT'S BEYOND THAT YOU MUST SEE

The football game is very close.
The score is tied at three.
The final pass is in the air.
What will the outcome be?

Whether on the field or on the bench,
Or sitting in the stands.
Whether as a coach or water boy,
Or marching with the bands.

It is you, my son, and only you
Who determines what shall be.
For this game is but one score in life.
It's beyond that you must see.

DAYS AT MUFORD HIGH

On a day much like today, at a high school very near,
There were four boys and a girl attending school.
The first, we'll call him Jim, was the hero every year.
He was the star of every sport . . . a mister cool.

Another we'll call Bob was most likely for success.
Every year he was a leader in his class.
The third guy was a party boy, the one they all called Jess.
He was a laugh-a-minute guy, but kinda crass.

It was Ernie who was odd and always seemed alone.
He wore funny clothes and never quite fit in.
The girl nobody knew, but we know her name was Joan.
Now, the story 'bout these folks we can begin.

Graduation came and passed, and as the years went by
The differences between them weren't so great.
Nobody seemed to care about their days at Muford High.
How they were back then was now quite out-of-date.

Jim learned that when he bragged of scores he then had made,
People yawned and most considered him a bore.
And even good ole' Jess had to learn himself a trade,
Cause the world was not just parties anymore.

Nobody cares today if Ernie couldn't get a date,
Or if Bob got all the votes at Muford High.
*It's what they are and what they learned that'll make 'em great,
Not what they were in childhood days gone by.*

To rest upon their laurels or to dwell on weaker traits
Will stop anyone from being fully grown.
The point this story makes is that all them can be great.
In fact, the ending has them working all for Joan.

FITTING IN

It's human nature to want to fit in,
But how low will you have to stoop?
What is the price of fitting in?
How important is the group?

These questions are very important, son,
So answer 'em before you say yes
To something a group expects you to do,
Or to someone you want to impress.

Tis the last of these questions that seems most hard,
Cause importance relates to time.
What now seems important to you or the group
Might later be worth not a dime.

Besides, my son, that group's gonna fade.
They'll grow and go their own way.
The man you become by saying no
Is the man with whom you will stay.

THE IMPRESSEE

If you must do or say something that's wrong
   To impress someone you see,
Then to be an impressor is not for you
   And neither's the impressee.

JUST LISTEN

If you want someone's friendship
Then while you both walk,
Just keep your mouth closed
And try not to talk.
   Just listen.

It is strange how people
Will think you so wise
When you don't say a thing,
But speak with your eyes
   And just listen.

Two ears and one mouth
Was for us a good start.
When used in proportion
We become twice as smart,
   So just listen.

AN EXPENSIVE SPORT

It's great to see you laugh and play,
    To know you're having fun.
But fun can be an expensive sport
    If it isn't wisely done.

Ask yourself some questions first,
    And use your common sense.
Is the fun you plan gonna be done
    At another person's expense?

Or maybe if you think a while,
    And the consequence you weigh,
You may learn it could be you
    That just might have to pay.

In any prison or graveyard
    I'll show you more than one
Who's there because he didn't weigh
    The cost of unwise fun.

Don't get me wrong, there is lots of fun
    A man can have today,
But the only fun that's really fun's
    When no one has to pay.

So think before you do that thing
    That is just for laughs, my son.
Cause fun does not make happiness,
    But happiness is lots of fun.

TO BE A MAN

What does it take to be a man,
  Just the age of twenty-one?
I've seen some folks of sixty years
  Not the man you are, my son.
If ever you judge one's manhood
  By the years that he's put in,
You may emulate some grown-up
  When a man he's never been.

What does it take to be a man?
  Is it hair upon your chest?
Or maybe some bulging muscles
  Will make you pass the test.
Those things may make a grown-up,
  But a man he may not be.
Don't ever judge one's manhood
  By the body that you see.

What does it take to be a man
  Like I know you wish to be?
Well, it's not just getting older
  Or acting out things you see.
Grown-up traits are visible traits.
  They are easy to achieve.
Manly traits are deeper within
  And harder to perceive.

IS HE A MAN?

Have you ever known a boy who brags a lot
About girls he's taken out?
Things he says happened while on his dates;
Those things that boy will shout.

I suppose he thinks it makes him a man,
But that's not what it's about.
In fact, the boy who does all the bragging
Must feel his manhood's in doubt.

When a boy boasts about all the notches
That he has carved in his belt,
It must mean his britches are just too big
For the manhood he's been dealt.

A true man respects the woman he's with
And holds their relationship dear.
Besides, my son, only a fool believes
Very much of what he might hear.

PLAYING WITH OUR FUTURE

Our greatest resource lies in our youth.
　That resource we must protect.
It isn't just up to us older folks
　To show our children respect.

When once on a date or with some friends,
　It could be something you did
That had an effect on some young person
　And changed the life of a kid.

How the world will be depends on its youth.
　That's a truth and not a myth.
When a young boy plays with other children,
　It's our future he's playing with.

THAT TEAR UPON YOUR CHEEK

Some teach the young boys
They should never cry.
The reason, they say,
Is a boy is a guy,
    And guys shouldn't be so weak.

Well, I've met many men
While crossing the oceans.
The surest of them
Will show their emotions.
    Feelings to men aren't unique.

It's mostly those men
Who are truly in doubt
Over what being a man
Is really about
    Who say crying is so weak.

So forget what you hear
About macho men,
And don't be ashamed
When you feel now and then
    That tear upon your cheek.

TOMORROW'S LEADER

Any boy can say yes to everything
And just drift along with the flow,
But the boy who will lead in years ahead
Is man enough now to say no.

NON-GROWING PAINS

A growing boy may see another
Who's exactly his own age
Who seems to be a whole lot older;
To have reached another stage.

It is true that some boys develop fast
And others develop slow.
But the race to manhood isn't determined
By how fast a body will grow.

. . . *Having passed through adolescence, the young adult carries both pride in his successes and scars from many hurts. Some have become men at this stage while others are still boys in a mature body. None are yet the men they will someday be.*

The young adult now has different pressures and concerns. Choosing a career, becoming "successful", buying a car, getting married, starting a family, paying bills, learning a trade and other such things now occupy his thoughts. Very often the young adult is still preoccupied with trying to "fit in" and prove himself to others. He often feels that lots of money will prove his "success" and that marrying an attractive woman will somehow prove his "manhood."

How is this young adult to know what will bring him true happiness? What is "success" and how is it achieved? What qualities are really important in a wife? What should his priorities be? How does he put life in perspective? . . .

WHAT'S THE SENSE?

No matter what kind of sense you have:
   Sense or scents or cents.
The kind of sense to cherish most
   Is good ole' common sense.

DOING

An education will make you smart.
It's something a man should prize.
But schooling, son, is just a start.
It's experience that makes one wise.

You can spend years with theories galore,
Looking through rose colored glasses.
But one year of doing will teach you more
Than a decade spent in classes.

AWESOME DECISION

What a wonderful thing, to be in love;
  To "know" that girl's for you.
But it is a shame so many young men
  Hurry so to say "I do."

It is true, my son, that charm can deceive;
  That beauty fades away.
It's the love for things that will always be
  That wise young men will weigh.

Does she have love and peace and self-control?
  Is she kind and full of joy?
Is she patient and good and faithful, too?
  Does she really love my boy?

If your answers are yes and you love her,
  Then once you decide to wed,
Why not wait one more year, just to make sure,
  Before those vows are said?

For better, for worse — In sickness or health.
  Your commitment is for life.
It's an awesome decision that any man makes
  The day he chooses a wife.

THE BETTER LIFE

Tis much better to live
in a tent all your life
Than to live in a mansion
with a nagging wife.

THE TURTLE AND YOU

There are many things that limit men
   And make an old man cry,
But none as sure as when he knows
   He didn't even try.

No man who tries can a failure be,
   At least not in my eyes.
The only man I'd call a failure
   Is the man who never tries.

Our life's much like the turtle's life,
   For if his moves you'll check,
He never takes one step ahead
   Til he first sticks out his neck.

PROCRASTINATION

The only thing between here
And your destination
Is that time-eating monster
called procrastination.

IT MUST BE WHAT THEY "ATE"

Successful men will innovate,
Originate and initiate.

They conjugate, congregate,
cogitate and meditate.

They incorporate, speculate,
consolidate and syndicate.

They coronate, inaugurate,
abdicate and dedicate.

They emancipate, liberate,
integrate and emigrate.

They legislate, adjudicate,
litigate and vindicate.

They investigate, estimate,
calculate and tabulate.

They medicate, inoculate,
sanitate and operate.

They titillate, infatuate,
stimulate and propagate.

They aviate, navigate,
fabricate and duplicate.

They cooperate, participate,
coordinate and tolerate.

They communicate, negotiate,
mediate and arbitrate.

They cultivate, excavate,
irrigate and compensate.

They appreciate, congratulate,
celebrate and elaborate.

They perforate, penetrate,
appropriate and captivate.

They educate, graduate,
concentrate and hesitate.

They regulate, delegate,
generate and terminate.

They reiterate, anticipate,
mitigate and simulate.

Others simply procrastinate.

THE CREATURE IN DISGUISE

There are conflicting rumors that are spreading around
About some kind of creatures that are roaming this ground.
There are big ones and small ones, they say, everywhere.
But just what they look like, no one is aware.

Some think they are mean, cause I've heard many cases
Where they jump up and slap folks right in their faces.
Yet victims never see 'em cause to this day they swear
That the illusive creatures just never were there.

If you don't grab 'em quick when they first come near
They will go like a flash and never reappear.
There are thousands of schools that train us to find 'em
And wonderful bounties for those who can bind 'em.

Rumors say they look small when coming your way,
But they look a lot bigger when going away.
They often wear disguises and hide in the dark.
To find them takes working, one man did remark.

I've heard of men hunting them all of their days.
Others just wait for them as if in a daze.
Some lucky folks do have them knock at their door,
But most the shy creatures knock once and no more.

Rumors conflict, but in one thing there's unity.
When the creatures were named, they were named opportunity.
So if you never see one, don't sit there and moan.
You can get off your backside and create your own.

CONTROL

Your future, your career,
Your happiness, too,
Cannot be controlled
Till you first control you.

. . . Like adolescence, the period of middleage is often one of crises. Some men are well on their way to fulfilling the dreams they had as a young man. Others are not. It is at this stage that some men begin looking back as much as ahead. Perhaps they're not where they wanted to be. Perhaps they have the career success they thought was so important, but family or health problems minimize the importance of that success.

Did they give up too much for the things they have? How do they find happiness now? What is really important? Have their values and/or priorities been wrong? How should they change their lives? How can they change?

Sadly, it is at this stage that many men first turn to the true values in life and begin to discover what is really important. Some reset their goals and become contented with less . . . only to find that they really have much more.

How were they to have known?

A PAIN IN THE NECK

Looking back causes a pain in the neck
For those who do it a lot.
"If I'da done this." or "If I'da done that."
Won't getcha anymore than you got.

TAKING YOUR MEDICINE

There are many things a man must accept . . .
　　Things in life that'll always exist.
There's weather and taxes and physical things,
　　But blame's at the top of the list.

Most will accept anyone's thanks,
　　And credit we're happy to claim.
But when things go wrong, how many folks
　　Are willing to accept the blame?

"It was Johnny's fault." or "I couldn't help it."
　　Or "Look what you made me do!"
Those are common phrases we hear every day.
　　Accepting the blame is taboo.

What about that mistake you recently made
　　For which you now feel shame?
Will you let it just fester and grow inside,
　　Or stand up and take the blame?

Keeping shame inside is like a bad disease.
　　It can make anyone feel sick.
Like a dose of medicine is blame, my son,
　　It's better if you take it quick.

It's easy to blame others for what goes wrong,
　　Or face the blame some later day.
But to stand up now and admit it's your fault
　　Is by far the wiser way.

VALUES & PRIORITIES

Every man has goals, dreams and aspirations. What seems to separate the happy men from the unhappy men is not so much whether dreams are fulfilled; nor does it seem to be material possessions, physical traits or intelligence level. Have you ever wondered how some can be so happy with what seems to be so little, or how some who appear to have so much manage to be so unhappy?

To better understand how true happiness can be achieved, perhaps one should explore what it is that makes men unhappy. Unhappiness always stems from a loss of some kind . . . a loss of something deemed important.

The most obvious type of loss is the more outward kind . . . the loss of a dream or desire that never materialized, the loss of affection or love from a friend or spouse, the loss of possessions, the loss of youth for an athlete, the loss of a loved one. Such losses, often unpreventable, will happen in every life. How we react is largely dependent on our perspective of life. That perspective is often determined by the priorities we establish for ourselves. If that thing that is lost is a high priority in our life, such a loss can be devastating.

What of the businessman who loses his fortune in a business transaction? What of the man who reaches middle-age only to realize that the "success" about which he always dreamed will simply never be? What of the young lover who loses his girl to another? What do they now have left? What were their priorities?

What are the material or external things you want in life? Will they bring you lasting happiness? Perhaps it is more pertinent to ask if you can have that happiness without those things. Do you own your dreams or do they own you? Where are these things in your priorities?

There are many things in life that cannot be taken away. The happiest of men keep these as their priorities. Others often give them away in pursuit of dreams they feel are more important. It is the loss of these things that will surely bring unhappiness.

One such loss is that of your pride, self-worth and self-esteem. The young man who turns to drugs, for instance, because "fitting-in" with some group is one of his top priorities will eventually think less of himself. Some of his self-esteem will vanish. When that group is gone, what is left? Should "fitting-in" have been a top priority? His convictions, his values and his self-esteem will some-day be far more important, but how was he to have known?

Another such internal and preventable loss is, perhaps, the number-one cause of unhappiness in our country . . . the loss of our inner peace. Hatred, jealousy, bitterness, envy, intolerance, spite and other such emotions can rob us of our inner peace and hence of our happiness.

Perhaps that happy man who appears to have so very little has more than meets the eye. Perhaps he kept those things that others gave away. Perhaps he kept his convictions and his values intact, thus keeping his self-esteem. Perhaps he kept his sense of humor and developed love for the people and beautiful things that sur-round him, thus keeping his inner peace. Perhaps these were his priorities.

A man with those priorities is free. He is free to seek all the dreams, material items and worldly pleasures he wishes without risk of them possessing him. He can care about all men, but no care will own him. He will suffer loss, sorrow, disappointment and sadness like other men, but he will emerge with his happiness and his sense of humor intact. Such a man is a blessed man.

DREAMS

People's dreams have made this land
A special place to live.
Hope and joy and goals for life
Are things a dream can give.

So dream, my son, but heed these words:
Dreams can spell disaster
When you stop smelling that tiny rose,
And dreams become your master.

THINGS

To seek your pleasure from things you own
Whether many things or few,
Can add spice to life and bring some joy
Until those things own you.

OVERLOOKED PLEASURES

The greatest of pleasures
For you and for me
Are often overlooked
Because they are free.

THE ROAD TO HAPPINESS

That illusive place called happiness
Is sought by many men.
Let's review the journey they make
And where those men have been.

Most men started on their journey
Quite early in their years.
Some tell me gruesome stories about
A road that's filled with tears.

They speak of fog that settled in
So they couldn't see ahead;
How some roads seemed completely blocked
By the waters storms had shed.

They talk of signs along the road
That led some men astray;
Of laughing fools at every turn
Who promise a better way.

Some took wrong turns, were lost for years.
Some never made it back.
It seemed the roads that looked most smooth
Were ones that went off-track.

I heard of times they had to tread
Where no road had been cut.
Of lonely, boring years they spent
Just plodding in a rut.

Some saw mirages just ahead . . .
Thought happiness was there.
But when they reached the spot they saw,
They found that spot was bare.

They told of bandits they couldn't see
    Who would rob them of their souls,
And men disguised as kindly friends
    Offering fruit in poison bowls.

No matter how tough the journey was
    Those arriving always said,
They learned to see in darkest of times
    And to find the light ahead.

When describing the road they all agreed
    That it went clear around.
It was the very same place they started
    That happiness was found.

Many years were wasted by some of those men
    They suffered needless strife,
Cause happiness is no destination, son,
    It's a daily way of life.

THE THIEF OF HAPPINESS

Think of cold and what it really is.
　Tis only the absence of heat.
It grows much easier for us to feel
　The more the warmth does retreat.
Hate is like cold; It cannot be felt
　Till something is taken away
It's absence of love that brings on hate.
　That is a heavy price to pay.

For instance, if one has genuine love
　For the things he does each day,
And also has love for every person
　Whom he meets along the way.
If he finds the good in everything
　And in every person, too,
That man with love is a happy man
　And his sorrows will be few.

Now, take that man and change his thoughts.
　Remove some love from him.
Do you think that man's still happy,
　Or is his life more grim?
You see, my son, hate is like cold.
　A bitter feeling it makes.
Some love must go before hate moves in,
　And that your happiness takes.

WEALTHY MEN

The men who have pride and peace of mind
And the respect of other men . . .

The men who say in their twilight years
That they'd do it all again . . .

The men who love the flowers and trees
And watching the animals play . . .

These are wealthy men, for what they have
Can never be taken away.

ABILITIES

If I could list for you, son, what skills to acquire . . .
The abilities I think are key.
The list I'd make would look something like this.
It's these that can make a man free.

The ability to:

Face disagreement without feeling disagreeable.
Be alone without feeling lonely.
Be doubted without having doubts.
Lose without suffering loss.
Try without feeling foolish.
Be judged without judging.
Own without being owned.
Care without caring too much.
Fail without being a failure.
Be lied about without dealing in lies.
Succeed without feeling superior.
Say no without fear of rejection.
Think well of yourself and not be bound
    by other's thoughts.
Wait and not be tired by waiting.
Pursue dreams without them pursuing you.
Love, yet not let love destroy you.
Choose friends without fear of not being chosen.
Help others without known reward.
Witness dishonesty, yet not be dishonest.
Be yourself and then be proud you were.

IN COMPARISON

When I graded myself from one to ten
Compared to others I know,
In every category someone was better.
My grades were always too low.

So I quit doing that and changed my ways.
I am happier now than then.
If I'm better today than I was before
I simply give myself a ten.

THE GIFT OF TIME

If every man received his pay
The day he was given birth,
The wise ones would invest it well
And build upon their worth.

The foolish men would waste their wealth
And squander their every cent,
Then someday beg for one more dime
Cause their fortune they have spent.

We did receive that gift at birth.
Our pay was precious time.
Since we never know how much we have,
Every minute should be prime.

Each day is like a dollar, son,
When you spend it, it is gone.
But when that day's invested wise,
Many great things it can spawn.

The rest of your life begins right now.
What a very special day!
Twenty-four hours for you to invest
So that every hour will pay.

THE TIME TILL THEN

If a year from now seems a long, long time,
   And next month seems far away,
Then tell me, son, where last month has gone,
   Why last year's like yesterday.

Patience is taught by the history of time;
   By taking a look at its past.
Like the days before that went fleeting by,
   The days ahead will go fast.

People think they can't wait till a week from now
   When a wonderful thing is foreseen,
But the very best part of a week from now's
   Seven days to enjoy in between.

YOUR LONG-TERM ADDRESS

It's strange how some will give such great care
To the house their body lives in,
Yet mistreat and abuse that marvelous place:
The body their soul is in.

Some spend their fortunes to buy a house.
It's a symbol of their wealth.
Such comforts mean little to any of them
If they've also spent their health.

So ponder this question: Where do you live?
But think before venturing a guess.
That number and street belong to a house.
Your body's your long-term address.

A SELF-ASSURING THOUGHT

If your luck is good, the day will come
    When you'll be old and grey.
Perhaps it's time you looked ahead
    To the thoughts you'll have that day.

You'll think of times you laughed so hard
    Your side began to ache,
And times you cried yourself to sleep,
    Your heart about to break.

The fun you had, mistakes you made,
    And dreams you had to chase.
The loves you lost, those childhood friends,
    That special little place.

All those thoughts you will have, my son,
    But none will be so blest
As that downright self-assuring thought
    That you did your very best.

A FRIEND'S FRIENDS

There's very little that'll stop a man's growth
  Or restrict his thinking more,
Than to limit his circle to those of one kind
  And to others shut the door.

Some very fine people whose paths you'll cross
  Won't be a bit like you.
They'll dress and act and look much different
  And not do the things you do.

Being their friend isn't always so easy.
  Others you know may object.
But in the end you'll broaden your circle
  And gain everybody's respect.

Even one who's a friend to everyone
  Won't have everyone as a friend,
But the man who's a friend to everyone
  Has many more friends in the end.

A GREAT MAN'S VIEW

We all can love the good times
  Or beauty in the sky above,
Or embrace a friend who helped us.
  That's the easy kind of love.

But what of the ones who bring us harm?
  Is there beauty in them, too?
Finding love for the ones who hurt us
  Is a difficult thing to do.

There are many things to understand.
  Many which we never will.
But always try hard to understand
  The ones who mean us ill.

Tis easy to hate or to judge those folks,
  To seek revenge or fight.
But conflict brings us certain grief,
  So why not set things right?

To understand such people as these
  Our eyes and ears won't do.
It's through a loving heart we must see
  To have a great man's view.

GREAT MEN

Great men are common men,
Born of kings or no.
They dine with the rich,
Mingle with the poor,
And those in between they know.

THE OTHER VIEW

Even small men have opinions.
   To them each issue's clear.
When another view is stated,
   Small men never hear.

Common men have opinions.
   They know that theirs is right.
When other views are spoken,
   They'll argue, even fight.

Great men also have opinions,
   But are not afraid to grow.
They listen with an open mind
   And learn what others know.

If you have respect for others' views
   And never shut them out,
You'll learn far more than issues, son,
   You'll learn what folks are about.

You needn't agree with everything said,
   But listen as close as you can,
For nothing will ever serve you more
   Than understanding fellow man.

THE SMALLEST MIND

The smallest of minds is the narrow mind,
  And notice what it abuts.
It is usually located just above
  A mouth that seldom shuts.

OF WHAT WE SPEAK

A great man speaks of ideals and truths.
Principles are his thrust.
He sees the good in everybody.
The great man we can trust.

The common man speaks of things and events,
Happenings, and not much more.
He picks his friends from one select group.
He's the guy we all know next door.

The lowly man speaks of other people,
Finding fault whenever he can.
He plays people against one another,
And that's not much of a man.

One can tell more by what a man speaks
Than the words that he utters may say.
His tongue is his brush, his words his palette,
And his portrait he paints every day.

CURSE OR GIFT

We split tiny atoms and land on the moon.
  We get energy out of a hole.
Yet the most powerful thing that we ever had
  Runs rampant and out of control.

  It's the most awesome weapon known to man.
  It's begun every war that time has span.
  It's injured more people and caused more pain
  Than the atomic bomb or the fighter plane.
  It causes despair. It causes deceit.
  It leads us astray and shows our conceit.
  It makes enemies and fabricates lies.
  It's often quite filthy and it terrifies.

If we could only control this thing
  That brings us all such disgrace,
It could do more good than anything else
  To make the world a better place.

  It forms beautiful music for us to hear.
  It carries our good news far and near.
  It can carry our love from city to city.
  It can make us feel pretty or make us seem witty.
  An integral part of most every college,
  It can educate us and give us knowledge.
  It can give us good taste and make us friends.
  It can guide our children and make amends.
  It can help us know what folks have to say.
  Millions of them are in use every day.

We should learn its power and learn its use,
  And learn it while we're young.
It's an awesome thing that we'd better control.
  That thing that's called a tongue.

ADVICE

Two very old men were homeless and hungry.
    A penny they had not one.
The first had taken all advice that was offered.
    The other had taken none.

The moral is not to close your ears,
    Or ignore what advice is about.
It's simply that you must trust in yourself
    When others remain in doubt.

NOTE: This book and its companion books, titled *"For My Daughter"* and *"For My Darling,"* are all original works by George E. Young and are offered for sale only through carefully selected retail outlets. For a list of outlets nearest you, please write to Young Interests, Inc., 41829 N. Deer Trail Rd., Cave Creek, AZ 85331.

Also, be on the lookout for Mr. Young's newest book, titled *"Growing Up Together."* Scheduled for its first printing in 1991, this new book is a must for any parent. Written entirely in prose, it will offer a candid and refreshing approach to common sense parenting.